Love in the City

Jerry Tilley

Published by Jerry Tilley, 2024.

LOVE IN THE CITY

First edition. August 6, 2024.

ISBN: 979-8227370105

Written by Jerry Tilley.

Table of Contents

Chapter 1: The Unexpected Meeting

Emma Mason's alarm buzzed insistently at 6:00 AM, pulling her from the depths of a dream. She groaned, reaching out to silence it, then lay in bed for a moment, staring at the ceiling. Today was going to be a big day. She had an important meeting that could make or break her career as a marketing executive at one of New York City's top firms.

She finally dragged herself out of bed and headed to the bathroom, splashing cold water on her face to wake up fully. The routine was always the same: a quick shower, a cup of strong coffee, and a scan through her emails before she dressed for work. Today, she chose a sharp, tailored suit, aiming to project confidence and professionalism.

As she applied her makeup, she thought about the presentation she would give later. It was a high-stakes pitch to a potential client who could bring significant revenue to the company. She had spent countless hours preparing, and now it was time to deliver.

Emma's apartment was a small but stylishly furnished space in Manhattan. It reflected her personality perfectly—neat, organized, and filled with little touches of creativity. A shelf of meticulously arranged books lined one wall, and a few pieces of modern art adorned the others. She glanced at a framed photograph of her family on the bedside table and smiled. Their support had always been a source of strength for her.

As she finished getting ready, Emma couldn't help but feel a mixture of excitement and nervousness. She had always been a high achiever, driven by a desire to succeed and make a name for herself in the competitive world of marketing. Today's meeting was a crucial step toward that goal.

By 8:00 AM, Emma was out the door, navigating the chaotic streets of New York City. The city was already buzzing with activity: honking cars, bustling pedestrians, and the ever-present hum of conversation. Emma loved the energy of the city, but today it added to her anxiety.

She glanced at her watch and quickened her pace. She couldn't afford to be late. As she dodged a group of tourists, her phone buzzed with a reminder of the meeting time. She took a deep breath, trying to steady her nerves. She had rehearsed her pitch a hundred times and knew it by heart.

The skyscrapers loomed overhead, casting long shadows across the sidewalks. Emma weaved through the crowd, her mind racing with last-minute details about the presentation. She mentally rehearsed her opening lines, picturing the faces of the clients she needed to impress.

As she approached a busy intersection, Emma's phone buzzed again. She glanced down at the screen, momentarily distracted. In that split second, she collided with someone, sending her coffee flying. "Oh no!" she exclaimed, looking up to see a man covered in coffee. He was tall, with a rugged look and a kind smile that seemed out of place in the midst of the chaos.

"I'm so sorry!" Emma said, flustered. "I wasn't watching where I was going."

The man, Jake, laughed it off. "It's alright. I needed a new shirt anyway," he said with a wink. "I'm Jake, by the way."

"Emma," she replied, feeling a strange mix of embarrassment and intrigue.

Jake Bennett was an artist living in a small loft in Brooklyn. His days were spent painting and sketching, always searching for inspiration in the bustling city around him. Today, he had decided to visit an art supply store in Manhattan to pick up some new materials for a project he was working on.

As he walked, he absorbed the sights and sounds of the city, finding beauty in the ordinary. The people, the architecture, the energy of the city—all of it fueled his creativity. He was deep in thought, planning his next piece, when he suddenly found himself drenched in coffee.

"Oh no!" he heard a woman exclaim. Jake looked down at his shirt, now stained with coffee, and then up at the woman who had bumped into him. She was clearly in a hurry, but there was something about her that caught his attention. Maybe it was the way she apologized, genuinely concerned, or the way her eyes met his with a mix of embarrassment and kindness.

"I'm so sorry!" she repeated, flustered. "I wasn't watching where I was going."

Jake laughed, trying to put her at ease. "It's alright. I needed a new shirt anyway," he said with a wink. "I'm Jake, by the way."

"Emma," she replied, her cheeks flushing slightly.

They stood there for a moment, caught in an unexpected connection. The world around them seemed to fade away as they exchanged a few more words. Emma explained she was on her way to an important meeting, and Jake wished her luck, genuinely hoping she'd do well. They both felt a spark, an unspoken understanding that this brief encounter was something special.

As Emma walked away, she couldn't help but glance back. Jake was still standing there, watching her with a smile. She felt her heart skip a beat, a feeling she hadn't experienced in a long time. She shook her head, trying to focus on the task ahead, but Jake remained in her thoughts.

Emma couldn't shake the encounter from her mind. She replayed it over and over as she made her way to the office. There was something about Jake that intrigued her. He seemed different from the other people she encountered daily.

Jake, on the other hand, was equally struck by Emma. He watched her walk away, wondering if he would ever see her again. As he continued to his art studio, he found himself inspired by the brief interaction, already thinking of how he could incorporate the experience into his next piece.

Arriving at his studio, Jake quickly changed out of his coffee-stained shirt and began sketching. The encounter had sparked a new idea, and he was eager to get it down on paper. He imagined Emma's face, her expression, and the moment they had shared. It was as if he could still feel her presence, and he wanted to capture that feeling in his art.

Emma, meanwhile, arrived at her office just in time for the meeting. She took a deep breath and stepped into the conference room, ready to present. Her colleagues greeted her with nods of encouragement, and she set up her materials.

The presentation went smoothly. Emma was in her element, confidently delivering her pitch and answering questions. The clients seemed impressed, and by the end of the meeting, she felt a wave of relief wash over her. Her hard work had paid off.

Throughout the day, Emma interacted with her colleagues, managing projects and addressing challenges as they arose. She was known for her dedication and attention to detail, qualities that had helped her rise through the ranks at the firm.

Despite the success of the meeting, Emma couldn't stop thinking about Jake. His image kept popping into her mind at the most unexpected times. She found herself wondering what he was doing, whether he was thinking about her too.

Meanwhile, Jake arrived at his art studio, a converted loft space filled with canvases, paints, and sketches. He had always been passionate about art, but the path hadn't been easy. Financial instability was a constant challenge, but he persevered, driven by his love for creating.

Today, he found himself distracted by thoughts of Emma. He replayed their encounter in his mind, her bright eyes and confident demeanor lingering in his thoughts. Inspired, he began sketching, hoping to capture the essence of their brief meeting.

As the day went on, Jake worked on several pieces, preparing for an upcoming gallery show. Despite the pressures of his career, he found solace in his art, losing himself in the process of creation.

As the evening approached, Emma returned home, exhausted but satisfied with her day's accomplishments. She poured herself a glass of wine and settled onto her couch, reflecting on the events of the day. Her mind kept drifting back to Jake, and she found herself wondering if their paths would cross again.

She called her best friend, Sarah, to recount the day's events. "You won't believe what happened this morning," she said, launching into the story of her coffee mishap and meeting Jake.

Sarah laughed. "Sounds like something out of a movie. Maybe it's fate."

Emma smiled, feeling a flicker of hope. "Maybe," she said softly.

Meanwhile, Jake was having a similar conversation with his friend and fellow artist, Mark. "I met someone today," he said, describing his encounter with Emma.

Mark grinned. "Sounds like she made quite an impression."

"She did," Jake admitted. "I just hope I get to see her again."

As Emma and Jake settled into their evening routines, both couldn't shake the feeling that their encounter was significant. Emma found herself daydreaming about Jake, imagining what it would be like to get to know him better. Jake, inspired by Emma, continued to pour his emotions into his art, hoping their paths would cross again.

Their lives continued, filled with the usual ups and downs, but the memory of their meeting lingered, a spark of possibility in the midst of their daily routines. Both hoped for another chance encounter, wondering what the future might hold.

Chapter 2: Sparks Fly

Jake Bennett stood in the middle of the gallery, taking a deep breath as he surveyed the room. The walls were adorned with his latest works, a collection he had poured his heart and soul into over the past year. Tonight was the opening of his solo exhibition, and the room buzzed with anticipation as guests began to arrive.

The gallery was a sleek, modern space in Manhattan with high ceilings and plenty of natural light. It was the perfect setting to showcase Jake's vibrant, emotional pieces. Each painting told a story, capturing moments of passion, struggle, and triumph. Jake had always believed that art should evoke a reaction, and he hoped tonight's guests would feel the same.

As he mingled with early arrivals, Jake couldn't help but feel a mix of excitement and nerves. This show was a significant milestone in his career. A successful opening could lead to more opportunities, more recognition, and the financial stability he desperately needed.

Emma Mason stepped out of the taxi, her heart racing with a mix of anticipation and curiosity. She had decided to attend the gallery opening on a whim, intrigued by the invitation she had received through a mutual acquaintance. As she walked towards the entrance, she couldn't shake the memory of her encounter with Jake that morning.

The gallery was already filling up with people, and Emma took a moment to appreciate the atmosphere. Soft music played in the background, and the air was filled with the low hum of conversation.

She felt a surge of excitement as she stepped inside, eager to see the art and, she admitted to herself, hoping to see Jake again.

Emma made her way through the crowd, pausing to admire the paintings. Each piece was unique, bursting with color and emotion. She could see the passion in every brushstroke, the intensity that Jake had described during their brief conversation. It was as if the paintings were speaking to her, drawing her in.

As Emma moved through the gallery, she spotted Jake across the room, engaged in conversation with a group of guests. He looked different tonight, more confident and self-assured. She hesitated for a moment, unsure if she should approach him, but then their eyes met, and he smiled.

"Emma, you made it!" Jake said, excusing himself from the group and walking over to her.

"Hi Jake," Emma replied, her heart fluttering. "I wouldn't have missed it. Your work is incredible."

Jake blushed slightly, clearly pleased by her compliment. "Thank you. It means a lot to hear that from you."

They stood there for a moment, the noise of the gallery fading into the background as they reconnected. The spark they had felt that morning was still there, even stronger now.

Jake offered to give Emma a tour of the gallery, and she eagerly accepted. As they walked from piece to piece, he explained the inspiration behind each painting, sharing stories of late nights in his studio and the emotions that had driven him to create.

Emma was captivated not just by the art, but by Jake's passion and vulnerability. He spoke with such honesty and openness, and she felt herself drawn to him more and more. They talked about their own lives, their dreams, and the challenges they had faced. It was as if they had known each other for years, not just a few hours.

"Your art is amazing, Jake," Emma said, stopping in front of a particularly striking piece. "I can see how much you put into it."

"Thank you, Emma," Jake replied, his eyes locking onto hers. "It means a lot coming from you. I'm really glad you're here."

As the evening went on, Emma and Jake found themselves sharing more personal stories. Emma opened up about her struggles to balance her demanding job with her personal life, and Jake talked about the financial uncertainties of being an artist. They discovered they had more in common than they had realized, and their bond grew stronger with each passing moment.

At one point, they found themselves standing on the gallery's balcony, looking out over the city. The night air was cool, and the city lights sparkled below them. It was a perfect moment, one that neither of them wanted to end.

"I feel like I've known you forever," Emma said softly, turning to Jake.

"Me too," Jake replied, taking her hand. "There's something about you, Emma. Something special."

As the gallery began to empty, Emma and Jake reluctantly said their goodbyes. They exchanged phone numbers, promising to see each other again soon. Emma left the gallery with a sense of excitement and anticipation, her mind racing with thoughts of Jake.

Jake too felt a renewed sense of hope and inspiration. Meeting Emma had been unexpected, but it felt right. He couldn't wait to see where this new connection would lead.

As Emma walked back to her apartment, she couldn't help but smile. Tonight had been magical, and she was eager to see what the future held for her and Jake.

Jake returned to his studio, his mind buzzing with inspiration. Meeting Emma had ignited a spark within him, and he couldn't wait to translate that energy into his art. He set up a new canvas and began to sketch, capturing the essence of their encounter.

Jake's creative process was intense and immersive. He worked late into the night, losing track of time as he painted. He thought about Emma, her smile, her laughter, and the way she had connected with his art. He wanted to create something that reflected the emotions he had felt, something that would capture the magic of their meeting.

As the hours passed, Jake's studio filled with the sounds of soft music and the smell of paint. By the time he finally stepped back to admire his work, the sun was beginning to rise. He felt a deep sense of satisfaction and accomplishment, knowing that he had created something truly special.

The next morning, Emma woke up feeling refreshed and excited. She had a busy day ahead at work, but she couldn't stop thinking about Jake. She checked her phone, hoping to see a message from him. When she found none, she decided to send him a quick text.

"Good morning, Jake. I had a wonderful time last night. Your art is incredible. Looking forward to seeing you again soon. - Emma"

Emma hit send and smiled, feeling a flutter of anticipation. She got ready for work, her mind filled with thoughts of Jake and the connection they had shared. As she made her way to the office, she felt a sense of excitement and optimism that had been missing from her life for a long time.

Jake woke up to the sound of his phone buzzing. He groggily reached for it and saw a message from Emma. His heart skipped a beat as he read her words, and a smile spread across his face. He quickly typed a response.

"Good morning, Emma. I had an amazing time too. Thank you for coming. Can't wait to see you again. - Jake"

Jake sent the message and lay back in bed, feeling a sense of contentment and excitement. He thought about the previous night, the conversations, and the connection he had felt with Emma. He knew that meeting her was something special, and he couldn't wait to see where it would lead.

Emma arrived at her office feeling more energized than she had in weeks. She greeted her colleagues with a smile and dove into her work, tackling her tasks with renewed enthusiasm. Her mind, however, kept drifting back to Jake.

During her lunch break, Emma found herself daydreaming about their next meeting. She wondered what they would do, what they would talk about. She felt a sense of excitement and anticipation, a feeling that had been missing from her life for a long time.

As the day went on, Emma's colleagues noticed her good mood. "You seem happy today," her friend and coworker, Lisa, remarked.

"I am," Emma replied with a smile. "I met someone special last night."

Lisa's eyes widened with interest. "Tell me more!"

Emma shared the story of her encounter with Jake, from their coffee mishap to the gallery opening. Lisa listened with rapt attention, her excitement mirroring Emma's.

"Sounds like a fairytale," Lisa said with a grin. "I'm so happy for you, Emma."

"Thanks, Lisa," Emma replied, feeling a warm glow of happiness. "I'm excited to see where it goes."

Jake spent the day in his studio, working on his latest piece. The inspiration from his encounter with Emma was still fresh in his mind, fueling his creativity. He painted with a sense of purpose and excitement, eager to capture the emotions he had felt.

Throughout the day, Jake found himself thinking about Emma. He replayed their conversations, their shared moments, and the connection they had felt. He couldn't wait to see her again, to learn more about her, and share more of himself.

As the sun set, Jake stepped back to admire his work. He felt a deep sense of satisfaction, knowing that he had created something special. He hoped that Emma would feel the same way when she saw it.

Jake sent Emma a quick text. "How's your day going? I've been thinking about you. - Jake"

Emma replied almost immediately. "My day's been great, thanks to you. Can't wait to see you again. - Emma"

Jake smiled, feeling a warmth in his heart. He couldn't wait to see Emma again, to continue their journey together.

Later that evening, Emma and Jake exchanged texts, setting up their next meeting. They decided to meet for dinner at a cozy little restaurant in the West Village, a place known for its intimate atmosphere and delicious food.

Emma felt a surge of excitement as she

Chapter 3: The First Date

Emma's excitement was palpable as she prepared for her first official date with Jake. She had spent the day thinking about him, their connection, and the potential for something special. As she stood in front of her closet, she carefully selected a dress that she knew Jake would love. It was simple yet elegant, reflecting her style perfectly.

Jake too was filled with anticipation and nerves. He wanted everything to be perfect to make their evening special. He had made reservations at a cozy restaurant known for its intimate atmosphere and delicious food. He dressed in a casual yet stylish outfit, hoping to impress Emma.

As the time for their date approached, both Emma and Jake felt a mix of excitement and nervousness. They exchanged a few texts, their messages filled with playful banter and genuine affection.

"Can't wait to see you tonight. - Emma"

"Me too. I have a feeling it's going to be amazing. - Jake"

Emma arrived at the restaurant first, feeling a flutter of nerves as she waited for Jake. She was seated at a small table near the window, the flickering candlelight adding to the romantic atmosphere. She sipped her water, glancing around the restaurant and wondering what the evening would hold.

A few minutes later, Jake arrived, his heart racing with anticipation. He spotted Emma and smiled, feeling a warmth spread through him. She looked stunning, her beauty taking his breath away.

"Hi Emma," Jake said, giving her a warm hug. "You look amazing."

"Hi Jake," Emma replied, her cheeks flushing. "You look great too."

They sat down, the initial nerves quickly melting away as they began to talk. The conversation flowed effortlessly, filled with laughter and shared stories. They talked about their lives, their passions, and their dreams for the future.

The food was delicious, each dish a delightful surprise. They shared their meals, savoring the flavors and the experience. Emma found herself getting lost in Jake's eyes, feeling a connection that went beyond words.

As the evening went on, they grew more comfortable, more open. They shared personal stories, their fears and hopes, their pasts and futures. It was a night of discovery, of connection, of falling in love.

After dinner, Jake suggested a walk in the nearby park. Emma eagerly agreed, feeling a sense of adventure and excitement. They strolled through the park, the night air cool and refreshing. The city lights sparkled around them, creating a magical atmosphere.

They walked hand in hand, talking about everything and nothing. Emma felt a sense of peace and contentment, a feeling she hadn't experienced in a long time. Jake too felt a deep connection to Emma, a sense of rightness in being with her.

At one point, they stopped by a small pond, the moonlight reflecting off the water. Jake turned to Emma, his eyes filled with emotion. "Emma, I know we haven't known each other long, but I feel a connection with you. Something special."

Emma's heart raced as she looked into Jake's eyes. "I feel it too, Jake. I don't know where this will go, but I'm excited to find out."

They stood there, holding hands, feeling the weight of their words. It was a moment of honesty, of vulnerability, of falling in love. As they continued their walk, they knew that this was just the beginning of their journey together.

As they walked back to Emma's apartment building, the air was filled with a sense of anticipation. They stood outside, reluctant to say goodbye. The night had been magical, and neither of them wanted it to end.

"Thank you for a wonderful evening, Jake," Emma said, her voice filled with genuine warmth.

"Thank you, Emma," Jake replied, his eyes locked onto hers. "I had an amazing time."

There was a moment of silence, filled with unspoken emotions. Jake stepped closer, his heart pounding. He gently cupped Emma's face in his hands and leaned in, their lips meeting in a tender, passionate kiss.

The kiss was electric, filled with a mix of desire and emotion. It felt like the culmination of all the feelings they had been building up throughout the evening. When they finally pulled apart, both were breathless, their eyes reflecting the intensity of the moment.

"Goodnight, Emma," Jake whispered, his voice filled with promise.

"Goodnight, Jake," Emma replied, her heart full.

As Emma watched Jake walk away, she felt a sense of exhilaration and hope. She knew that this was just the beginning of something special.

The next morning, Emma woke up with a smile on her face. She felt a sense of excitement and anticipation, a feeling that had been missing from her life for a long time. She checked her phone and saw Jake's message, her heart skipping a beat.

She got ready for work, her mind filled with thoughts of Jake. As she made her way to the office, she couldn't help but replay the events of the previous night in her mind. The dinner, the walk, the kiss—it had all been perfect.

Emma felt a renewed sense of energy and optimism as she tackled her tasks for the day. Her colleagues noticed her good mood, and she couldn't help but share her excitement with them.

During her lunch break, Emma received another message from Jake. "How about dinner again this weekend? - Jake"

Emma quickly replied. "I'd love that. Looking forward to it! - Emma"

The anticipation of their next meeting filled Emma with a sense of joy and excitement. She couldn't wait to see Jake again, to continue exploring the connection they had.

Jake woke up feeling energized and inspired. The evening with Emma had been everything he had hoped for and more. He felt a deep connection to her, a sense of rightness in being with her.

Fueled by the emotions of the night, Jake set up a new canvas and began to paint. He wanted to capture the essence of their evening, the magic of their connection. He painted with a sense of purpose, each stroke filled with passion and emotion.

As the hours passed, Jake lost himself in his work. The studio was filled with the soft sounds of music and the smell of paint. By the time he finally stepped back to admire his work, the sun was beginning to rise. He felt a deep sense of satisfaction, knowing that he had created something truly special.

Jake sent Emma a quick text. "Last night was amazing. I can't stop thinking about you. - Jake"

Emma replied almost immediately. "Me too, Jake. It was perfect. - Emma"

Jake smiled, feeling a warmth in his heart. He couldn't wait to see Emma again, to continue their journey together.

As the weekend approached, both Emma and Jake found themselves eagerly anticipating their next date. They exchanged texts throughout the week, their messages filled with playful banter and genuine affection.

Emma spent the evening before their date preparing, choosing a dress that she knew Jake would love. She felt a mix of excitement and nervousness, wondering what the evening would hold.

Jake too was filled with anticipation. He wanted everything to be perfect, to make their evening special. He made reservations at a romantic restaurant, one that he knew Emma would love.

Emma arrived at the restaurant, her heart racing with anticipation. She spotted Jake waiting for her, his face lighting up with a smile as she approached.

"Hi Jake," Emma said, giving him a warm hug. "It's great to see you."

"Hi Emma," Jake replied, his eyes filled with affection. "You look beautiful."

They sat down, the initial nerves quickly melting away as they began to talk. The conversation flowed effortlessly, filled with laughter and shared stories. They talked about their week, their thoughts, and their feelings for each other.

The food was delicious, each dish a delightful surprise. They shared their meals, savoring the flavors and the experience. Emma found herself getting lost in Jake's eyes, feeling a connection that went beyond words.

As the evening went on, they grew more comfortable, more open. They shared personal stories, their fears and hopes, their pasts and futures. It was a night of discovery, of connection, of falling in love.

After dinner, Jake suggested a walk by the waterfront. Emma eagerly agreed, feeling a sense of adventure and excitement. They strolled along the water, the night air cool and refreshing. The city lights sparkled around them, creating a magical atmosphere.

They walked hand in hand, talking about everything and nothing. Emma felt a sense of peace and contentment, a feeling she hadn't experienced in a long time. Jake too felt a deep connection to Emma, a sense of rightness in being with her.

At one point, they stopped by a small pier, the moonlight reflecting off the water. Jake turned to Emma, his eyes filled with emotion. "Emma, I know we haven't known each other long, but I feel a connection with you. Something special."

Emma's heart raced as she looked into Jake's eyes. "I feel it too, Jake. I don't know where this will go, but I'm excited to find out."

They stood there, holding hands, feeling the weight of their words. It was a moment of honesty, of vulnerability, of falling in love. As they continued their walk, they knew that this was just the beginning of their journey together.

Emma returned to her apartment, still buzzing with excitement from the evening. She poured herself a glass of wine and settled onto her couch, replaying the events of the night in her mind. She felt a warmth in her heart that she hadn't felt in a long time. The connection she had with Jake was undeniable, and she couldn't help but wonder where it would lead.

As she sipped her wine, Emma pulled out her journal and began to write. She often used journaling as a way to process her thoughts and emotions, and tonight was no different. She wrote about the

As she sipped her wine, Emma pulled out her journal and began to write. She often used journaling as a way to process her thoughts and emotions, and tonight was no different. She wrote about the dinner, the walk, and the feelings that had stirred within her. She found herself smiling as she described Jake, his passion, and the way he made her feel.

Jake returned to his studio, his mind buzzing with inspiration. The evening with Emma had been everything he had hoped for and more. He felt a deep connection to her, a sense of rightness in being with her.

Fueled by the emotions of the night, Jake set up a new canvas and began to paint. He wanted to capture the essence of their evening, the magic of their connection. He painted with a sense of purpose, each stroke filled with passion and emotion.

As the hours passed, Jake lost himself in his work. The studio was filled with the soft sounds of music and the smell of paint. By the time he finally stepped back to admire his work, the sun was beginning to rise. He felt a deep sense of satisfaction, knowing that he had created something truly special.

Jake sent Emma a quick text. "Last night was amazing. I can't stop thinking about you. - Jake"

Emma replied almost immediately. "Me too, Jake. It was perfect. - Emma"

Jake smiled, feeling a warmth in his heart. He couldn't wait to see Emma again, to continue their journey together.

Over the next few days, Emma and Jake found themselves eagerly anticipating their next meeting. Their text exchanges became more frequent and intimate, filled with playful banter and heartfelt confessions. They shared their daily experiences, their thoughts, and their dreams, building a deeper connection with each passing day.

One evening, Jake sent Emma a text that made her heart flutter. "I've been thinking about you all day. Can't wait to see you again this weekend. - Jake"

Emma replied with a smile. "Me too, Jake. I'm counting down the days. - Emma"

Chapter 4: Building Connections

Emma and Jake were now officially a couple, and their excitement for each other grew with every passing day. The early stages of their relationship were filled with discovery, laughter, and a deepening bond that neither had experienced before. They were eager to learn more about each other, to understand their histories, their dreams, and their fears.

Emma decided it was time to introduce Jake to her friends and family. She was nervous but confident that they would love him just as much as she did. She planned a small dinner party at her apartment, inviting her closest friends and her parents.

Jake arrived early to help Emma set up. He brought flowers for Emma and a bottle of wine for her parents. As they worked together to prepare the meal, their camaraderie and affection for each other were evident.

Emma's friends arrived first. Lisa, her best friend and coworker, was the first to arrive. She hugged Emma and then turned to Jake, her eyes sparkling with curiosity.

"So you're the famous Jake," Lisa said with a grin. "Emma hasn't stopped talking about you."

Jake laughed, feeling a bit bashful. "I hope it's all good things."

"All good things," Lisa confirmed, giving Emma a knowing look.

As more friends arrived, Jake found himself feeling more and more at ease. He enjoyed the lively conversations and the warm, welcoming atmosphere. Emma's friends were all kind and engaging, and he could see why she valued them so much.

When Emma's parents arrived, Jake felt a pang of nervousness. He wanted to make a good impression, to show them that he was serious about their daughter. Emma's mother, Karen, was warm and affectionate, while her father, Robert, was more reserved but kind.

"Jake, it's a pleasure to meet you," Karen said, giving him a hug. "Emma has told us so much about you."

"Likewise," Jake replied, smiling warmly. "Thank you for having me."

The dinner was a success. The food was delicious, the conversation flowed effortlessly, and Jake felt a deep sense of belonging. Emma's parents were impressed by his warmth and sincerity, and her friends quickly accepted him as part of their group.

After everyone had left, Emma and Jake sat together on the couch, reflecting on the evening.

"That went well, didn't it?" Emma said, leaning against Jake.

"It did," Jake agreed, wrapping his arm around her. "Your friends and family are wonderful. I can see why you're so close to them."

"I'm glad you think so," Emma replied, smiling up at him. "They really liked you."

Jake felt a warmth in his heart, knowing that he had made a good impression. He was excited to introduce Emma to his world, to share his friends and family with her.

The following weekend, Jake planned a get-together at his loft, inviting his closest friends and family. He was excited to introduce Emma to the people who meant the most to him.

Emma arrived at Jake's loft, feeling a mix of excitement and nervousness. She had heard so much about Jake's friends and family, and she wanted to make a good impression.

Jake's loft was a cozy, creative space, filled with his artwork and personal touches. Emma admired the way he had transformed the space into a reflection of his personality and creativity.

Jake's friends were the first to arrive. Mark, his best friend and fellow artist, greeted Emma with a warm hug. "It's great to finally meet you, Emma," he said. "Jake talks about you all the time."

"Nice to meet you too, Mark," Emma replied, smiling. "I've heard a lot about you as well."

As more friends arrived, Emma felt herself relaxing and enjoying the evening. Jake's friends were all creative and passionate, and she felt inspired by their conversations and their warmth.

When Jake's parents arrived, Emma felt a pang of nervousness. She wanted to make a good impression, to show them that she was serious about their son. Jake's mother, Linda, was warm and welcoming, while his father, Tom, was more reserved but kind.

"Emma, it's a pleasure to meet you," Linda said, giving her a hug. "Jake has told us so much about you."

"Likewise," Emma replied, smiling warmly. "Thank you for having me."

The evening was a success. The food was delicious, the conversation flowed effortlessly, and Emma felt a deep sense of belonging. Jake's parents were impressed by her warmth and sincerity, and his friends quickly accepted her as part of their group.

After everyone had left, Jake and Emma sat together on the couch, reflecting on the evening.

"That went well, didn't it?" Jake said, leaning against Emma.

"It did," Emma agreed, wrapping her arm around him. "Your friends and family are wonderful. I can see why you're so close to them."

"I'm glad you think so," Jake replied, smiling up at her. "They really liked you."

Emma felt a warmth in her heart, knowing that she had made a good impression. She was excited to continue building their connection, to share more of her world with Jake.

As Emma and Jake continued to build their relationship, they found themselves supporting each other's dreams in new and meaningful ways. Emma encouraged Jake to pursue his dream of opening his own gallery, offering her expertise and connections in the marketing world. Jake, in turn, supported Emma's ambitions in her career, offering his unwavering encouragement and love.

One evening, as they sat together in Jake's loft, Emma shared an exciting opportunity that had come her way. "I've been offered a promotion at work," she said, her eyes shining with excitement. "It's a big step up, and it means a lot more responsibility, but it's also a huge opportunity."

Jake's face lit up with pride. "That's amazing, Emma! You deserve it. I know you'll do great."

"Thank you, Jake," Emma replied, feeling a warmth in her heart. "I'm a little nervous, but I'm also excited. It's a chance to really make a difference."

"You'll be amazing," Jake said, squeezing her hand. "And I'll be here to support you every step of the way."

Emma smiled, feeling a deep sense of gratitude for Jake's support. She knew that with him by her side, she could take on any challenge.

Jake too was pursuing his dreams with renewed vigor. With Emma's encouragement, he began to make serious plans for opening his own gallery. He reached out to contacts in the art world, began scouting locations, and worked tirelessly on his art.

One afternoon, as they sat together in Jake's studio, he shared his progress with Emma. "I've found a potential location for the gallery," he said, showing her some photos. "It's a great space, and I think it could be perfect."

Emma looked at the photos, feeling a sense of excitement for Jake. "It looks amazing, Jake. I can see your art there. It's going to be incredible."

"Thank you, Emma," Jake replied, his eyes shining with determination. "I couldn't have done this without your support."

Emma felt a deep sense of pride and love for Jake. She knew that together they could achieve anything.

As Emma and Jake continued to build their relationship, they faced challenges and obstacles that tested their bond. They navigated the ups and downs of their careers, the pressures of their personal lives, and the complexities of their relationship.

One evening, as they sat together in Emma's apartment, Jake shared a difficult situation he was facing. "I've hit a bit of a roadblock with the gallery," he said, his voice filled with frustration. "There are some legal and financial hurdles that I didn't anticipate, and it's been really stressful."

Emma felt a pang of empathy for Jake. She knew how much this dream meant

to him and how hard he had been working to make it a reality. She reached out and took his hand, giving it a reassuring squeeze.

"Jake, I'm so sorry you're dealing with this," Emma said softly. "But I know you're strong and determined. You'll find a way through this. And I'm here to help in any way I can."

Jake looked into Emma's eyes, feeling a sense of relief and gratitude. "Thank you, Emma. Your support means everything to me."

Over the next few weeks, Emma and Jake worked together to overcome the challenges they faced. Emma used her business acumen to help Jake navigate the legal and financial aspects of opening his gallery, while Jake continued to create new artwork and build connections in the art community. Their teamwork and mutual support brought them even closer together.

Chapter 5: Conflicts and Misunderstandings

As Emma and Jake's relationship deepened, they inevitably faced conflicts and misunderstandings. They were both passionate and driven individuals, and sometimes their ambitions and busy schedules led to tension.

One evening, after a particularly long and stressful day at work, Emma returned home feeling exhausted and overwhelmed. She had been dealing with a difficult client and was feeling the pressure of her new responsibilities. When she saw that Jake hadn't yet arrived for their planned dinner, she felt a surge of frustration.

She sent him a quick text: "Hey, where are you? I thought we were having dinner tonight."

A few minutes later, Jake replied: "Sorry, Emma. I got caught up at the studio. I'll be there soon."

Emma sighed, feeling her frustration grow. She had been looking forward to spending time with Jake, and now it felt like he was putting his work ahead of their relationship. When Jake finally arrived, Emma's emotions boiled over.

"Jake, this isn't the first time you've been late," Emma said, her voice tinged with irritation. "I understand you're busy, but I need to know that I'm a priority too."

Jake looked taken aback, clearly not expecting the confrontation. "Emma, I'm really sorry. I didn't mean to make you feel unimportant. I just got caught up in my work."

"I know you're passionate about your art, and I love that about you," Emma replied, her voice softening. "But I need to feel like we're in this together, that our relationship is a priority for both of us."

Jake took a deep breath, realizing the weight of Emma's words. "You're right, Emma. I've been so focused on the gallery that I haven't been as present as I should be. I promise I'll do better."

Emma felt a sense of relief and hope. She knew that conflicts were a part of any relationship, but it was how they handled them that mattered. "Thank you, Jake. I appreciate that. I just want us to be a team."

As they talked through their feelings, Emma and Jake found a renewed sense of understanding and commitment. They agreed to communicate more openly about their needs and to make time for each other, even amidst their busy schedules.

Their relationship continued to grow stronger, but they knew that there would be more challenges ahead. They were determined to face them together, supporting each other through the ups and downs.

Chapter 6: Navigating Career Challenges

As Emma settled into her new role at work, she found herself facing increasing pressure and demands. The promotion had brought new responsibilities and higher expectations, and Emma was determined to prove herself. She worked long hours, often bringing work home and sacrificing her personal time.

Jake was also pushing himself to the limit, juggling the demands of creating new artwork, managing the gallery's preparations, and building relationships in the art community. Despite their best efforts to balance their careers and relationship, the strain began to take its toll.

One evening, after a particularly grueling day, Emma sat at her desk, surrounded by piles of documents and her laptop open to yet another work email. She felt a wave of exhaustion and frustration wash over her. She hadn't seen Jake in days, and she missed him terribly.

As if sensing her thoughts, her phone buzzed with a message from Jake: "Hey, how's your day going? Miss you. - Jake"

Emma smiled, feeling a warmth in her heart. She quickly replied: "It's been a rough day. I miss you too. Can we make time for each other this weekend? - Emma"

Jake's response was immediate: "Absolutely. Let's plan something special. You deserve a break. - Jake"

The promise of spending time with Jake lifted Emma's spirits. She knew that their relationship was worth fighting for, even amidst the challenges they faced. As the weekend approached, she looked forward to the chance to reconnect and recharge.

Jake planned a surprise getaway for Emma, taking her to a quaint bed-and-breakfast in the countryside. It was the perfect escape from the hustle and bustle of the city, a chance to relax and enjoy each other's company.

As they arrived at the charming inn, Emma felt a sense of peace wash over her. The air was crisp and fresh, and the surrounding landscape was a picturesque mix of rolling hills and vibrant autumn foliage.

"This is perfect, Jake," Emma said, taking his hand. "Thank you for this."

"You deserve it, Emma," Jake replied, pulling her close. "I've missed you."

Their weekend was filled with laughter, relaxation, and intimate moments. They went on long walks, explored the nearby town, and enjoyed quiet dinners by the fireplace. It was a chance to reconnect, to remind themselves of why they had fallen in love in the first place.

As they sat together on the porch of the inn, watching the sunset, Emma felt a renewed sense of hope and determination. "Jake, I know our careers are important, but I don't want us to lose sight of what we have. Let's make a promise to always prioritize our relationship."

Jake nodded, his eyes filled with love and commitment. "I promise, Emma. We'll make it work, no matter what."

Their weekend getaway was a turning point for Emma and Jake. They returned to the city with a renewed sense of purpose and a deeper commitment to each other. They continued to face the challenges of their careers, but they did so as a team, supporting and uplifting each other every step of the way.

Chapter 7: Celebrating Milestones

As the months passed, Emma and Jake found themselves celebrating several important milestones in their relationship and careers. They had grown closer than ever, their bond strengthened by the challenges they had faced and overcome together.

Emma's hard work at the marketing firm paid off, and she was recognized with a prestigious industry award. The accolade was a testament to her dedication and talent, and it opened up new opportunities for her career.

Jake's gallery opening was a resounding success. The event was well-attended, and his artwork received rave reviews. He sold several pieces, and the gallery quickly gained a reputation as a must-visit destination for art lovers.

To celebrate their achievements, Emma and Jake decided to throw a joint celebration party at the gallery. They invited their friends, family, and colleagues, creating an evening filled with joy, laughter, and love.

The gallery was beautifully decorated, with Jake's artwork providing a stunning backdrop. Guests mingled, enjoying delicious food and drinks, and celebrating the successes of the couple they had come to admire and support.

Emma and Jake stood together, surrounded by their loved ones, feeling a deep sense of gratitude and happiness. They had come so far, and their journey was only just beginning.

During a quiet moment, Emma turned to Jake, her eyes shining with emotion. "I'm so proud of us, Jake. We've accomplished so much together."

Jake smiled, pulling her into a loving embrace. "I couldn't have done it without you, Emma. You've been my rock, my inspiration."

As they shared a tender kiss, surrounded by the people who meant the most to them, Emma and Jake knew that they had found something truly special. They had built a life together, one filled with love, passion, and unwavering support.

Their celebration was a testament to their journey, a reminder of the power of love and the strength of their bond. As they looked forward to the future, they knew that whatever challenges lay ahead, they would face them together, united by their love and commitment to each other.

Chapter 8: Exploring the World Together

With their careers on track and their relationship stronger than ever, Emma and Jake decided to embark on a new adventure: traveling the world together. They had always dreamed of exploring new places, experiencing different cultures, and creating unforgettable memories.

Their first destination was Paris, the city of love. They spent their days wandering through the charming streets, visiting iconic landmarks, and indulging in delicious cuisine. They visited art galleries, inspired by the rich history and beauty of the city.

One evening, as they stood on the balcony of their hotel room, overlooking the twinkling lights of the Eiffel Tower, Jake turned to Emma with a look of pure happiness. "This is everything I've ever dreamed of, Emma. Thank you for sharing this with me."

Emma smiled, feeling a deep sense of contentment. "Thank you, Jake. This is just the beginning of our adventures together."

Their travels took them to many other beautiful destinations: the romantic canals of Venice, the breathtaking landscapes of the Swiss Alps, the vibrant streets of Tokyo, and the stunning beaches of Bali. Each place brought new experiences, new memories, and a deeper connection between them.

As they explored the world together, Emma and Jake found that their love grew stronger with each passing day. They supported each other through the challenges of travel, celebrated the joys of discovery, and cherished the quiet moments of simply being together.

Their journey was filled with laughter, adventure, and a sense of wonder. They took countless photos, capturing the magic of their travels and the

beauty of their love. They met new friends, learned new languages, and immersed themselves in the cultures of the places they visited. Each destination brought them closer together, deepening their bond and strengthening their commitment to each other.

One day, while exploring the ancient ruins of Machu Picchu, Jake had a special surprise for Emma. As they stood on a mountaintop, gazing out at the breathtaking view, Jake turned to Emma, his heart pounding with anticipation.

"Emma, there's something I've been wanting to ask you," Jake said, reaching into his pocket.

Emma's eyes widened as Jake pulled out a small velvet box and got down on one knee. "Jake..."

"Emma, you are the love of my life, my best friend, and my greatest adventure. Will you marry me?"

Tears filled Emma's eyes as she looked at Jake, her heart overflowing with love. "Yes, Jake. Yes, a thousand times yes!"

Jake slipped the ring onto Emma's finger, and they embraced, both overcome with emotion. The other tourists around them cheered, and Emma and Jake shared a kiss that sealed their promise to each other.

Their engagement marked the beginning of a new chapter in their lives. They continued their travels, now planning their wedding and dreaming of their future together. They knew that no matter where life took them, they would always have each other.

Chapter 9: Giving Back to the Community

As Emma and Jake planned their wedding, they also felt a growing desire to give back to the community. They had been blessed with so much love and support, and they wanted to make a difference in the lives of others.

They decided to start a charitable foundation focused on supporting young artists and providing educational opportunities for underprivileged children. Emma used her marketing expertise to raise awareness and funds for their cause, while Jake offered art workshops and mentorship programs.

The foundation quickly gained traction, and Emma and Jake found themselves deeply fulfilled by their work. They saw the impact they were making, helping young people discover their talents and pursue their dreams.

One of their first projects was to renovate a local community center, turning it into a vibrant space for art and education. They organized fundraising events, rallied volunteers, and worked tirelessly to bring their vision to life.

The grand opening of the community center was a joyous occasion. Emma and Jake stood together, surrounded by the children and families they had helped, feeling a profound sense of accomplishment.

"This is what it's all about," Jake said, looking at Emma with pride. "Making a difference, one step at a time."

Emma nodded, her heart full. "I'm so proud of us, Jake. We're building something beautiful together."

Their foundation continued to grow, and Emma and Jake became known not only for their professional achievements but also for their generosity and commitment to giving back. They inspired others to get involved, creating a ripple effect of kindness and support.

Chapter 10: The Journey Continues

As their wedding day approached, Emma and Jake felt a mix of excitement and anticipation. They had chosen a beautiful vineyard as the location for their wedding, a place that held special meaning for both of them. It was where they had celebrated their first anniversary and where Jake had painted one of his most beloved pieces.

The vineyard was transformed into a magical setting, with twinkling lights, lush flowers, and a backdrop of rolling hills. Friends and family gathered from near and far to celebrate the love that had brought Emma and Jake together.

On the morning of their wedding, Emma and Jake each took a moment to reflect on their journey. Emma sat in a quiet corner of the vineyard, writing a letter to Jake. She poured her heart into the words, expressing her love, gratitude, and excitement for their future.

Jake, meanwhile, stood in front of a mirror, adjusting his tie and thinking about the woman he was about to marry. He felt a wave of emotion as he recalled all the moments that had led them to this day—their first meeting, the challenges they had faced, and the love that had grown stronger with each passing day.

As Emma walked down the aisle, her eyes locked onto Jake's, and she felt a surge of love and joy. Jake's heart swelled as he watched her approach, knowing that he was the luckiest man in the world.

The ceremony was filled with heartfelt vows, tears of joy, and the loving support of their friends and family. Emma and Jake exchanged rings, sealing their commitment to each other.

"I promise to love you, support you, and be your partner in all things," Emma said, her voice filled with emotion.

"And I promise to cherish you, to stand by your side, and to love you with all my heart," Jake replied, his eyes shining with tears.

As they shared their first kiss as husband and wife, the guests erupted in applause, and Emma and Jake knew that this was just the beginning of their lifelong adventure together.

The reception was a joyous celebration, filled with laughter, dancing, and heartfelt toasts. Emma and Jake danced under the stars, surrounded by the people who had supported them on their journey.

Later that evening, as they sat together on a blanket, watching the stars, Emma felt a sense of peace and contentment. "This is perfect, Jake. I couldn't have asked for a better day."

"It really is," Jake agreed, pulling her close. "I love you, Emma. I can't wait to spend the rest of my life with you."

"I love you too, Jake," Emma replied, her heart full. "Here's to our future, and all the adventures that lie ahead."

Chapter 11: Embracing Parenthood

A few years after their wedding, Emma and Jake decided to start a family. They were excited about the prospect of becoming parents and sharing their love and experiences with a new generation. The journey to parenthood was filled with anticipation, joy, and a few challenges along the way.

Emma and Jake were overjoyed when they discovered they were expecting their first child. They spent months preparing for the arrival of their baby, decorating the nursery, reading parenting books, and attending prenatal classes. Their friends and family were thrilled for them, offering support and advice as they navigated this new chapter in their lives.

The day their baby was born was one of the happiest moments of Emma and Jake's lives. They welcomed a beautiful baby girl, whom they named Lily. Holding her for the first time, they felt an overwhelming sense of love and responsibility.

"She's perfect," Emma whispered, tears streaming down her face.

"She really is," Jake agreed, his heart swelling with pride. "I can't believe she's ours."

As they settled into their new roles as parents, Emma and Jake discovered the joys and challenges of raising a child. They cherished the quiet moments, like rocking Lily to sleep or watching her take her first steps. They also faced the sleepless nights and the worries that came with being new parents.

Through it all, Emma and Jake supported each other, their bond growing even stronger. They found joy in the small moments, like Lily's first smile or her infectious laughter. They shared the responsibilities of parenting, ensuring that they each had time to pursue their passions while also being present for their daughter.

One evening, as they sat together in the nursery, watching Lily sleep, Emma turned to Jake. "I feel so blessed, Jake. We have a beautiful family, and I couldn't ask for more."

Jake smiled, taking her hand. "I feel the same way, Emma. Our journey together has been incredible, and I can't wait to see what the future holds for us and Lily."

As the years passed, Emma and Jake continued to build their family and their careers. They supported each other's dreams, celebrated each other's successes, and faced life's challenges together. They were a team, united by their love and their commitment to each other and their family.

Chapter 12: Building a Family

As their family grew, Emma and Jake found themselves navigating the joys and challenges of parenthood. They welcomed a second child, a baby boy named Max, and their home was filled with the sounds of laughter, play, and the occasional sibling squabble.

Emma and Jake were dedicated parents, ensuring that Lily and Max had a loving and supportive environment in which to grow. They balanced their careers with their family life, often taking turns to be present for important milestones and activities.

They also made time for their own relationship, recognizing the importance of nurturing their bond amidst the demands of parenthood. They planned regular date nights, went on family vacations, and found moments of quiet connection whenever they could.

One summer, they decided to take a family trip to a beach house, creating memories that would last a lifetime. They spent their days building sandcastles, playing in the waves, and enjoying the simple pleasures of being together.

As they sat around a bonfire one evening, roasting marshmallows and sharing stories, Emma felt a deep sense of contentment. "This is perfect," she said, looking around at her family. "I wouldn't trade this for anything."

Jake nodded, his heart full. "Me neither, Emma. Our family is everything to me."

Their journey as parents was filled with both challenges and triumphs. They faced the sleepless nights, the tantrums, and the worries that came with raising children. But they also experienced the joys of watching Lily and Max grow, discovering their unique personalities and talents.

Through it all, Emma and Jake remained committed to each other and to their family. They knew that their love and partnership were the foundation on which their family was built, and they worked hard to keep that foundation strong.

As the years went by, Emma and Jake found themselves reflecting on their journey. They had built a beautiful life together, filled with love, laughter, and countless memories. They were proud of the family they had created and excited for the future.

Chapter 13: Deepening the Connection

Emma and Jake's relationship continued to deepen as they navigated the various stages of their lives together. They supported each

other through the ups and downs, always finding ways to reconnect and strengthen their bond. Their love was a constant, a source of comfort and joy that carried them through the challenges they faced.

As their children grew older, Emma and Jake found themselves with a bit more time to focus on their own relationship. They started taking trips together again, exploring new places and revisiting old favorites. These trips were a chance to reconnect, to remind themselves of the adventure and romance that had brought them together in the first place.

One particularly memorable trip was to Italy, where they spent two weeks exploring the beautiful countryside, visiting art museums, and indulging in delicious food and wine. They stayed in a charming villa, surrounded by vineyards and olive groves, and spent their days wandering through picturesque villages and relaxing by the pool.

One evening, as they sat on the terrace watching the sunset, Jake took Emma's hand. "Emma, I feel so lucky to have you in my life. Every day with you is a gift."

Emma smiled, her heart full. "I feel the same way, Jake. Our journey together has been incredible, and I can't wait to see what the future holds."

They toasted to their love, their family, and the many adventures still to come. The trip was a beautiful reminder of the connection they shared and the importance of taking time to nurture their relationship.

Back at home, Emma and Jake continued to support each other's dreams and aspirations. Emma took on a new role at work, one that allowed her to have more flexibility and spend more time with her family. Jake's gallery continued to thrive, and he found new ways to give back to the community through his art.

They also made a point of staying involved in their children's lives, attending school events, supporting their hobbies, and spending quality time together as a family. They wanted to ensure that Lily and Max grew up feeling loved, supported, and encouraged to pursue their own passions.

Chapter 14: The Next Chapter

As Emma and Jake approached their fifteenth wedding anniversary, they decided to celebrate with a special event. They planned a vow renewal ceremony, inviting their closest friends and family to join them in reaffirming their commitment to each other.

The ceremony was held at the vineyard where they had gotten married, a place that held so many beautiful memories for them. The setting was perfect, with twinkling lights, lush flowers, and a backdrop of rolling hills.

Emma wore a simple yet elegant dress, and Jake looked dashing in a tailored suit. They exchanged heartfelt vows, reflecting on their journey together and the love that had grown stronger with each passing year.

"I promise to continue loving you, supporting you, and being your partner in all things," Emma said, her voice filled with emotion.

"And I promise to cherish you, to stand by your side, and to love you with all my heart," Jake replied, his eyes shining with tears.

As they shared a kiss, their guests erupted in applause, and Emma and Jake knew that this was just the beginning of the next chapter in their lives together.

The celebration that followed was filled with laughter, dancing, and heartfelt toasts. Emma and Jake danced under the stars, surrounded by the people who had supported them on their journey.

Later that evening, as they sat together on a blanket, watching the stars, Emma felt a sense of peace and contentment. "This is perfect, Jake. I couldn't have asked for a better day."

"It really is," Jake agreed, pulling her close. "I love you, Emma. I can't wait to spend the rest of my life with you."

"I love you too, Jake," Emma replied, her heart full. "Here's to our future, and all the adventures that lie ahead."

Chapter 15: Planning for the Future

As Emma and Jake looked ahead to the future, they began to think about the legacy they wanted to leave for their children and the community. They had accomplished so much together, and they wanted to ensure that their impact would continue to be felt for generations to come.

They decided to expand their charitable foundation, increasing their efforts to support young artists and provide educational opportunities for underprivileged children. They also established scholarships in their names, offering financial assistance to students pursuing careers in art and marketing.

Emma and Jake also began to think about their own future and what they wanted to achieve in the years to come. They set new goals for their careers, their family, and their personal growth, always supporting each other and encouraging each other's dreams.

One evening, as they sat together in their living room, Emma turned to Jake with a thoughtful expression. "Jake, what do you see for our future? What do you want to achieve in the next ten, twenty, thirty years?"

Jake smiled, taking her hand. "Emma, I want to continue doing what we love. I want to create more art, help more people, and build a life that we're proud of. But most importantly, I want to do it all with you by my side."

Emma felt a surge of love and gratitude for Jake. "I feel the same way. Whatever the future holds, I know we'll face it together."

They spent the evening dreaming and planning, mapping out their goals and aspirations. They knew that the future was full of possibilities, and they were excited to see where their journey would take them.

Chapter 16: Embracing Parenthood Again

A few years later, Emma and Jake found themselves contemplating the idea of expanding their family once more. They loved being parents and cherished the time they spent with Lily and Max. The thought of adding another child to their family filled them with excitement and joy.

After discussing it with each other and with Lily and Max, Emma and Jake decided to try for another baby. They were thrilled when they discovered that Emma was expecting, and they eagerly prepared for the arrival of their third child.

The pregnancy was a joyful time for their family. Lily and Max were excited about becoming older siblings, and they helped Emma and Jake prepare the nursery and gather baby supplies. The anticipation and excitement were palpable as they counted down the days until the baby's arrival.

The day their baby was born was one of the happiest moments of their lives. They welcomed a beautiful baby boy, whom they named Ethan. Holding him for the first time, they felt an overwhelming sense of love and gratitude.

"He's perfect," Emma whispered, tears streaming down her face.

"He really is," Jake agreed, his heart swelling with pride. "I can't believe he's ours."

As they settled into their new roles as parents of three, Emma and Jake discovered the joys and challenges of raising a larger family.

They cherished the quiet moments, like rocking Ethan to sleep or watching him interact with his older siblings. They also faced the sleepless nights and the worries that came with being parents once again.

Through it all, Emma and Jake supported each other, their bond growing even stronger. They found joy in the small moments, like Ethan's first smile or his infectious laughter. They shared the responsibilities of parenting, ensuring that they each had time to pursue their passions while also being present for their children.

One evening, as they sat together in the nursery, watching Ethan sleep, Emma turned to Jake. "I feel so blessed, Jake. We have a beautiful family, and I couldn't ask for more."

Jake smiled, taking her hand. "I feel the same way, Emma. Our journey together has been incredible, and I can't wait to see what the future holds for us and our children."

Chapter 17: A Legacy of Love

As Emma and Jake's children grew, they focused on instilling in them the values of love, kindness, and generosity. They wanted Lily, Max, and Ethan to understand the importance of giving back and making a positive impact on the world.

They involved their children in their charitable foundation, teaching them about the importance of helping others and supporting those in need. They organized family volunteer days, participated in community events, and encouraged their children to pursue their own passions and interests.

One summer, the family decided to embark on a humanitarian trip to a developing country, where they worked on building schools and providing educational resources for local children. The experience was transformative for the entire family, deepening their understanding of the world and their commitment to making a difference.

As they returned home, Emma and Jake felt a renewed sense of purpose and determination. They knew that their legacy would be one of love, compassion, and service to others.

Chapter 18: Nurturing Growth and Change

As the years went by, Emma and Jake continued to nurture their relationship, their family, and their community. They faced new challenges and embraced new opportunities, always supporting each other and growing together.

They also took time to reflect on their journey and the lessons they had learned along the way. They had built a beautiful life together, filled with love, laughter, and countless memories. They were proud of the family they had created and excited for the future.

One evening, as they sat together on their porch, watching the sunset, Emma turned to Jake with a thoughtful expression. "Jake, what do you think has been the most important lesson we've learned on this journey?"

Jake smiled, taking her hand. "I think it's that love is the foundation of everything. It's what has carried us through the challenges and brought us so much joy. And it's what will continue to guide us in the future."

Emma nodded, feeling a deep sense of gratitude for Jake and their journey together. "I agree. Love is the most powerful force in the world, and I'm so grateful to have you by my side."

As they sat together, watching the stars appear in the night sky, Emma and Jake knew that their journey was far from over. They had many more adventures, challenges, and joys ahead of them, and they were ready to face them together, united by their love and commitment.

54

Chapter 19: Embracing New Adventures

With their children growing up and becoming more independent, Emma and Jake found themselves with more time to explore new adventures and opportunities.

They decided to embark on a series of new adventures, both individually and as a couple, rekindling their sense of wonder and exploration.

One of their first new adventures was taking up sailing. They had always loved the ocean, and the idea of learning to sail excited them both. They enrolled in sailing lessons, spending weekends out on the water, learning the ropes and enjoying the tranquility and beauty of the sea. It was a new challenge, but they faced it together, supporting each other and growing closer in the process.

Their sailing adventures took them to many beautiful places along the coast, and they made new friends in the sailing community. It became a shared passion, a way to relax and escape from the stresses of everyday life. They often took the kids with them, creating unforgettable family memories on the water.

As they embraced new hobbies and experiences, Emma and Jake also found themselves rediscovering old passions. Emma returned to painting, setting up a small studio in their home where she could work on her art. Jake encouraged her, often joining her in the studio with his own creative projects. They found joy in creating together, sharing ideas and inspiring each other.

Jake continued to expand his gallery, curating new exhibitions and supporting emerging artists. He also began to experiment with new artistic mediums, pushing the boundaries of his creativity. Emma was his biggest supporter, always encouraging him to explore new ideas and take risks.

Their children, too, were growing and thriving. Lily was excelling in school and developing her own passion for writing, while Max showed a keen interest in science and technology. Ethan, the youngest, was full of energy and curiosity, always eager to learn and explore. Emma and Jake encouraged their children's interests, providing them with the resources and support they needed to pursue their dreams.

Chapter 20: Celebrating the Golden Years

As Emma and Jake entered their golden years, they found themselves reflecting on the incredible journey they had shared. Their love had grown and evolved, weathering the storms of life and emerging stronger and more beautiful with each passing year.

They decided to celebrate their fiftieth wedding anniversary with a grand celebration, inviting friends and family from all over to join them in marking this momentous occasion. The event was held at the same vineyard where they had gotten married and renewed their vows, a place that held so many precious memories.

The vineyard was beautifully decorated, with twinkling lights, lush flowers, and a backdrop of rolling hills. Friends and family gathered to celebrate the love that had brought Emma and Jake together and sustained them through the years.

As they stood together, surrounded by their loved ones, Emma and Jake felt a deep sense of gratitude and joy. They had built a life filled with love, laughter, and countless memories. They had supported each other through the highs and lows, always finding strength in their love and commitment.

During the celebration, Emma and Jake took a moment to address their guests, expressing their gratitude and sharing their reflections on their journey.

"Fifty years ago, we made a promise to each other," Emma began, her voice filled with emotion. "A promise to love, support, and cherish each other, no matter what. And looking back, I can say with certainty that we've kept that promise."

Jake nodded, his eyes shining with tears. "Emma, you are my best friend, my partner, and the love of my life. Our journey together has been more wonderful than I ever could have imagined. And I look forward to many more years of love and adventure with you."

Their guests erupted in applause, and Emma and Jake shared a tender kiss, sealing their promise once again.

The celebration continued with dancing, laughter, and heartfelt toasts. Emma and Jake danced under the stars, surrounded by the people who had supported them on their journey. It was a night filled with love, joy, and the promise of many more beautiful moments to come.

As they sat together, watching the stars, Emma felt a deep sense of peace and contentment. "This is perfect, Jake. I couldn't have asked for a better life."

"It really is," Jake agreed, pulling her close. "I love you, Emma. Always and forever."

"I love you too, Jake," Emma replied, her heart full. "Here's to our future, and all the adventures that lie ahead."

Epilogue: A Legacy of Love

Emma and Jake's love story continued to inspire those around them. Their children, Lily, Max, and Ethan, grew up to be kind, compassionate, and successful individuals, each pursuing their own dreams and passions. They carried with them the values of love, kindness, and generosity that Emma and Jake had instilled in them.

Emma and Jake's charitable foundation continued to thrive, making a positive impact on countless lives. They remained active in their community, always finding ways to give back and support those in need.

As they looked back on their journey, Emma and Jake felt a deep sense of pride and fulfillment. They had built a life filled with love, laughter, and countless memories. They had faced challenges together, supported each other through the highs and lows, and created a beautiful legacy of love.

Their love story was a testament to the power of love, commitment, and partnership. It was a reminder that, no matter what challenges life may bring, love can conquer all.

Emma and Jake's journey was far from over. They continued to embrace new adventures, celebrate life's moments, and cherish the love that had brought them together. Their story was a beautiful example of a life well-lived, a love well-loved, and a journey well-traveled.

As they sat together, watching the sunset, Emma turned to Jake with a smile. "Jake, we've had an incredible journey, haven't we?"

Jake smiled, taking her hand. "We have, Emma. And it's not over yet. Here's to many more adventures, my love."

"Here's to us," Emma replied, her heart full. "Always and forever."

And so, Emma and Jake continued their journey, hand in hand, their hearts forever intertwined. Their love story was a beautiful symphony, a testament to the power of love and the magic of a life shared with the one you love.

Also by Jerry Tilley

Saga of the Northern Star
The Lost City Chronicles
The Painter's Apprentice
The Pharaoh's Shadow
Empire of Sand
Love in the City
Mindful Minds: A Journey to Mental Health and Well-Being
Smart Money